SEASONS SEASONS SEASONS SEASONS

WINTER

Moira Butterfield

Illustrated by Helen James

Smart Apple Media

Published by Smart Apple Media
2140 Howard Drive West, North Mankato, MN 56003

Designed and illustrated by Helen James

Photographs by Corbis (Craig Lovell, Joe McDonald, Richard Hamilton Smith,
Craig Tuttle, Kennan Ward, Staffan Widstrand, WildCountry, Haruyoshi
Yamaguchi, Michael S. Yamashita)

Printed and bound in Thailand

Library of Congress Cataloging-in-Publication Data

Butterfield, Moira.
Winter / by Moira Butterfield.
p. cm. — (Seasons)
ISBN 1-58340-617-4
1. Winter—Juvenile literature. I. Title.

QB637.8.B86 2005
508.2—dc22   2005042574

First Edition

9 8 7 6 5 4 3 2 1

Contents

All about winter   4

My winter, your winter   6

Winter's coming   8

Winter weather   10

Winter garden   12

On a winter farm   14

Winter wild animals   16

The toughest ones   18

Winter stories   20

Winter parties   22

Paint the winter   24

Make a piece of winter   26

Be a winter scientist   28

Words to remember   30

Index   32

All about winter

Winter is a season, a time of year that can bring shivers, long, dark nights, and crunchy snow.

The sun gives us life. Without it, there would be no animals or plants on our planet.

Our year

The sun is a huge, fiery ball of burning gas that gives us warmth and light. Earth travels around the sun. It takes one year to go all the way around.

Earth words

The two halves of Earth are called the northern and southern hemispheres. While one has winter, the other has summer. The area around the middle of Earth is called the equator.

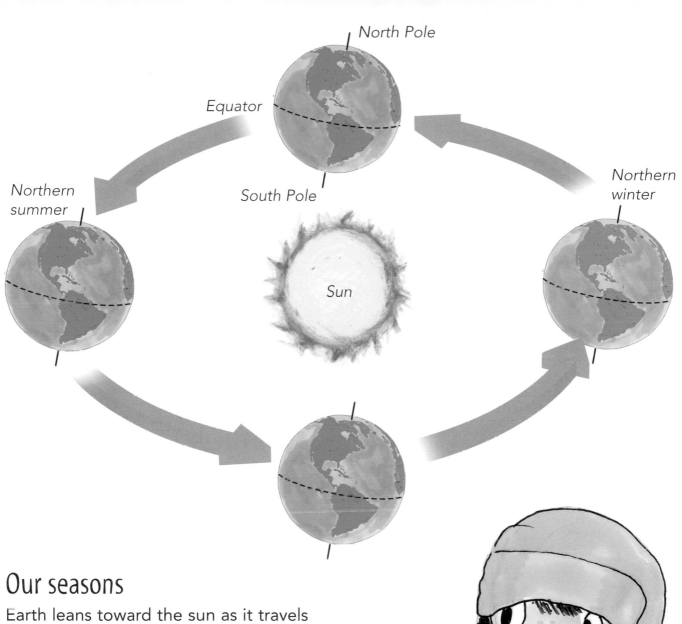

North Pole

Equator

South Pole

Northern summer

Sun

Northern winter

Our seasons

Earth leans toward the sun as it travels around it. The half closest to the sun has summer, while the other half has winter. So as Earth gradually turns around, the seasons change.

Worst winters

The sun's rays are weakest at the far northern and southern parts of Earth, called the poles. The poles have the coldest winters in the world.

My winter, your winter

Winter does not come at the same time for everyone. While you shiver in the winter cold, someone on the other side of the world could be sunbathing!

Winter north and south

In the northern half of Earth, winter comes in December, January, and February. In the southern half, winter comes in June, July, and August.

What about the middle?

In countries along the equator, it is hot year-round. There is no winter or summer there. Places near the equator have wet and dry seasons instead.

Days and nights

As Earth travels around the sun, it spins in space like a top. It takes 24 hours to spin once. First one side faces the sun, then the other, giving us days and nights. In the winter, days are shorter, and nights are longer.

Around the equator, there are wet and dry seasons instead of summer and winter.

Some parts of the world, such as parts of North America and northern Europe, have cold, snowy winters.

Some parts of the world, such as Australia, have rainy, cool winters, rather than lots of snow.

Dark all day

The North Pole, at the far north of the world, looks like land, but in fact it is frozen sea. In the winter, it is dark all day and all night there, and the temperature falls so low that the sea freezes over for many miles around.

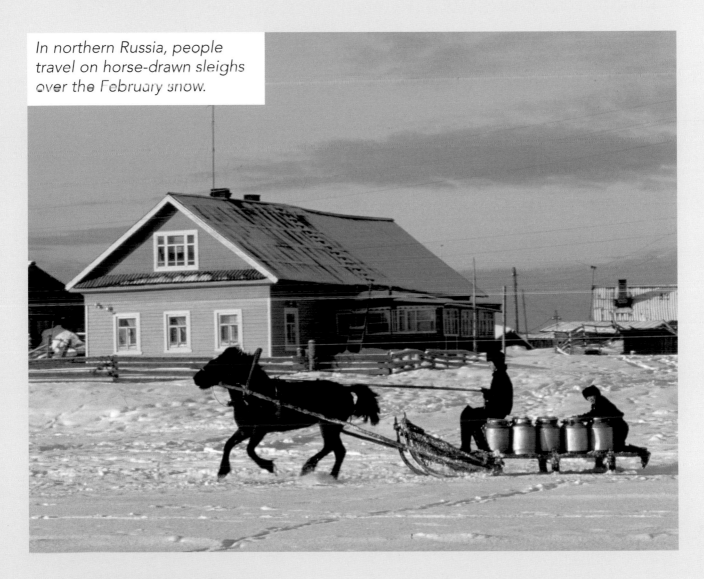

In northern Russia, people travel on horse-drawn sleighs over the February snow.

Colder than a freezer

At the far south of the world, there is an area of land called Antarctica. It is so cold there that the land is always covered in ice. In the winter, it is dark all day and all night. The sea turns to ice around the land, and the temperature is colder than a freezer.

Winter's coming

When winter is coming, the weather grows colder, and the nights last longer. Watch for these winter signs.

Birds leave

A lot of birds leave winter lands for somewhere warmer. You may see them flying overhead in big flocks on their journey away from the cold. You see fewer animals in the winter. Small insects die, and other creatures hide away from the cold.

Bare trees

Look down and you will see fewer plants than in the summer. As the weather grows colder, plants stop growing.

Look up and you will see deciduous trees (trees that lose their leaves) with bare branches.

Can you feel winter?

You can feel winter coming because the temperature falls outside. We measure temperature with a thermometer. Colored liquid inside squeezes up a thin tube as it gets warmer, and falls down the tube as it gets colder. Numbers along the tube measure how far up or down the liquid gets.

These numbers show the temperature, measured in degrees Fahrenheit (°F) or degrees Celsius (°C).

Winter goose bumps

When skin is cold, little pimples called goose bumps appear. Tiny muscles under your skin tighten, making the hairs on your skin stand on end. Your body wants the hairs to trap warm air around you.

Shivery winter

When you feel cold and start to shiver, it's your body's way of trying to warm you up. Your muscles tighten and relax quickly to make more warmth inside you. Then it's time to put on warm winter clothes!

Winter weather

Water freezes when its temperature drops below 32 °F (0 °C). That's why some parts of the world have winter ice and snow.

All about snow

When water freezes, it makes tiny crystals. In a cold winter cloud, these crystals form and then bang into each other to create snowflakes. Each snowflake is made up of more than 50 separate crystals stuck together.

Snow can be powdery or thick, slushy or dry, depending on how cold the weather is.

Snowflakes are hexagonal, which means they have six sides.

Snow patterns

Snowflakes have a beautiful patterned shape that can be seen under a microscope. Every snowflake has a different pattern. All snowflakes have six sides.

Winter frost

When the weather grows very cold, water vapor in the air turns to ice crystals called frost. Frost settles on the ground, plants, windows, and even spider webs. The ice crystals crunch when you walk over them.

Bad blizzards

Snowfall in the winter can make people's lives very difficult. Snowdrifts can block roads and make travel much harder and more dangerous. A really heavy snowstorm is called a blizzard.

Heavy snowfall can block roads.

Winter garden

In cold winter weather, plants stop flowering and growing. They wait for warmer days to return.

Saving water

Plants suck up water from the ground through their roots. In the winter, this gets harder because the ground freezes. Plants must use less water, so they stop growing and may die down to the ground, ready to shoot up again in the spring.

Deciduous trees lose their leaves in the winter.

Leaves that lose water

Flat, wide leaves (called broad leaves) lose a lot of water. It evaporates out into the air through tiny leaf holes called pores. To save water, broad-leaved trees lose their leaves in the winter. They are called deciduous trees.

Winter buds

In the winter, a deciduous tree has no leaves, but it does have winter buds on its branches. Inside each little bud are new leaves and flowers ready for next year. As soon as the weather gets warmer, the bud will swell and unfold.

Trees have winter buds on their branches.

Leaves like needles

Trees that keep their leaves all year are called evergreen. Their leaves are often shaped like thin needles. These leaves lose hardly any water through evaporation, so the trees can safely keep them through the winter.

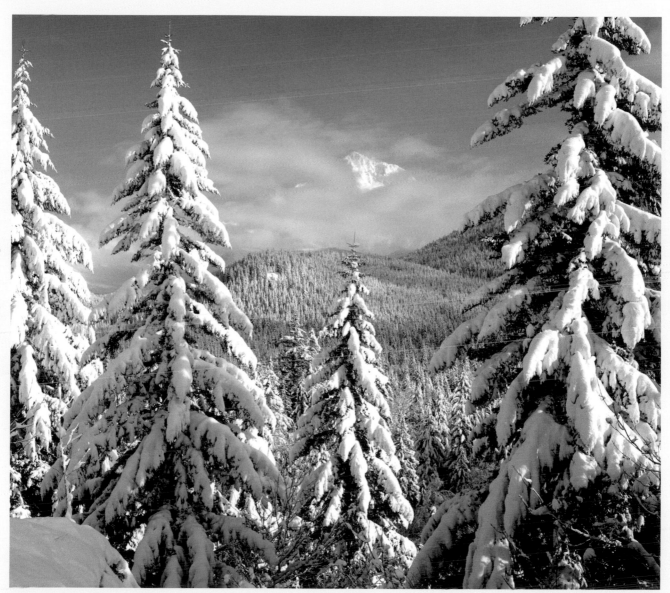

Shaped for snow

Conifers are evergreen trees that are good at growing in cold, snowy places. Their branches slope downward because that makes it easy for snow to slip off. Otherwise, a heavy winter snowfall could easily break off branches.

On a winter farm

In the winter cold, a farmer's fields seem quiet and empty, but there are still plenty of farm jobs to do.

Changing the soil

It might look as though nothing is going on in the fields, but something does happen to the soil in the winter. When it freezes and thaws, the top layer breaks into smaller pieces. That makes it easier to plant in spring.

Feeding the animals

There is not enough fresh grass for farm animals to eat in cold winter places. Instead, farmers feed them hay made from grass cut on the farm earlier in the year. The hay is stored in bundles called bales.

Feeding people

In snowy places, there are no fresh crops for people to eat. In the past, people ate food they had stored earlier in the year, such as grain made into bread. Today, many people simply eat food brought in from other warmer parts of the world.

14

Staying inside

In a harsh winter, the weather is too cold for cattle to stay outside. Instead, they are kept inside a barn. Every day, the farmer makes sure they are well fed and that their living areas are kept clean.

Woolly and tough

Sheep can stay outside because their woolly coats keep them warm. They eat hay put out by the farmer. In the mountains of Peru in South America, farmers keep alpacas. They have shaggy coats that are good for making wool.

Alpacas in the snowy Andes mountains. They stay warm because of their thick, shaggy coats.

Winter wild animals

In a cold winter, it's hard for wild animals and birds to survive. There isn't much food around, and it's difficult to keep warm.

Finding winter food

Predators, or hunting animals, search for winter food, but it's hard because many of the creatures they eat in the summer disappear in the winter. Creatures such as foxes go into towns to look for food among human trash.

Saving winter food

Some creatures gather a food store to eat during the winter. Squirrels and mice hoard food such as nuts and acorns, which they gather in the fall. These little animals huddle together in their dens to keep themselves warm.

Foxes may go to towns to search for food in the winter.

Winter fur

In snowy, cold places, furry animals often grow thicker fur to keep them warm through the winter months. Some animals, such as rabbits and weasels, change the color of their fur to blend in with the snowy background.

Good-night!

Some animals, such as bears and bats, hibernate in the winter. Bats gather in caves, where it is cool and damp. Sometimes they return to the same perch year after year.

Bears look for a warm, dry place to sleep in the winter.

The toughest ones

Imagine surviving a freezing winter in the Arctic or Antarctic. Some animals brave the snowstorms, and some leave for a warmer winter home.

See you in the spring

Many polar creatures migrate, traveling away from winter storms to somewhere warmer. Caribou (also called reindeer) travel south from the Arctic in huge herds of more than 100,000 animals.

I'm staying

Many birds leave the northern Arctic in the winter, but a few stay and put up with the cold. The white snowy owl stays to catch any small rodents that venture out. It also eats any dead animals it spots in the snow.

Shaggy musk oxen

Musk oxen stay put in tough Arctic winter conditions. They have long, shaggy coats to keep them warm. They look for mosses to eat in places where the wind has blown the snow away.

Polar bear hunters

Lone male polar bears roam the frozen winter sea ice of the far north, hoping to catch a seal when it comes up to breathe through a hole in the ice. Female polar bears hide in a den dug in a snowdrift. They give birth to twins during the winter.

Cozy underground

Small rodents called lemmings move around in underground burrows beneath the Arctic snow. They eat underground plant shoots to keep themselves alive.

Tough insects

In Antarctica, it can be –75 °F (–59 °C) in July. Only a few creatures can survive. Tiny insects called mites and springtails stay alive trapped in the ice. They have a substance called antifreeze in their blood that stops them from freezing solid.

Winter stories

There are legends about the seasons all over the world. Here are some winter stories.

An Iroquois Native American legend

The mighty god of all the winds was called Gaoh. He lived up in the sky. He summoned Earth's creatures to help him with his work, and a giant bear named Yaogah answered his call. "You shall be the freezing north wind," Gaoh commanded the bear, and he tethered Yaogah outside the north door of his home.

When the north wind blows, the Iroquois say that the bear is prowling in the sky. They say that Gaoh has unleashed Yaogah, and the bear's icy breath makes the world freeze.

An Inuit legend of the far north

This tale explains why the sea of the far north is icy. One day a famous Inuit hero named Kivioq was in his kayak when a storm blew him to a land he had never seen before. This was the home of an evil sorceress, who tricked humans into staying at her house and then killed them.

A friendly spirit warned Kivioq, and he escaped just in time, rowing out to sea in his kayak. The sorceress was so angry that she turned the water to ice, but Kivioq still managed to escape.

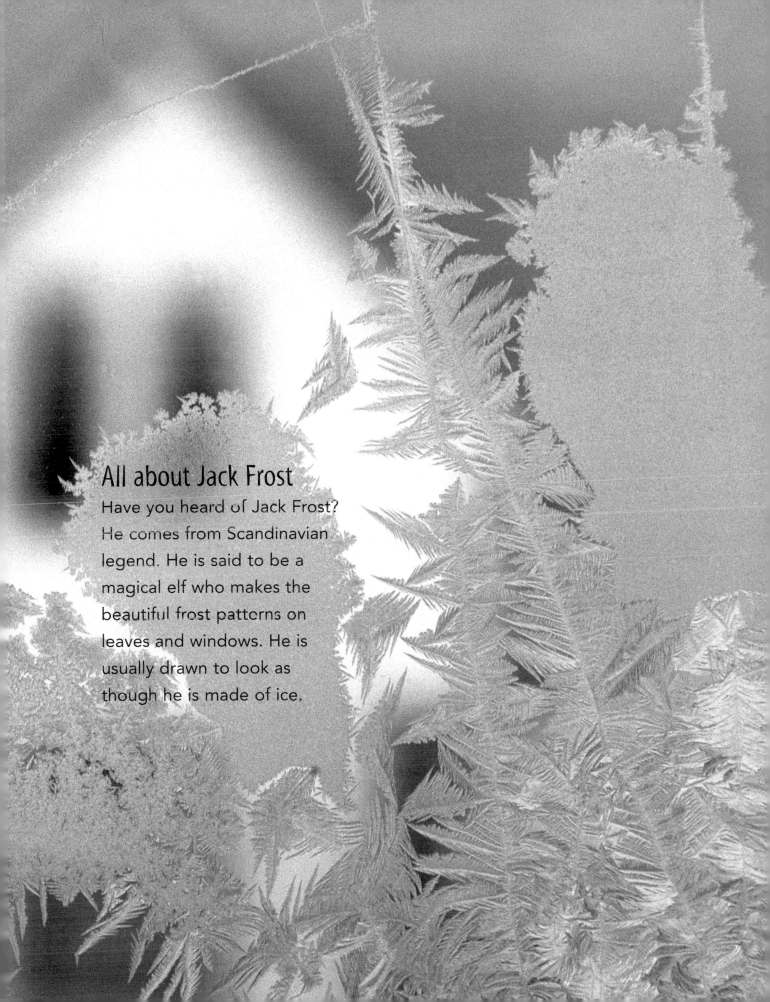

All about Jack Frost

Have you heard of Jack Frost?
He comes from Scandinavian
legend. He is said to be a
magical elf who makes the
beautiful frost patterns on
leaves and windows. He is
usually drawn to look as
though he is made of ice.

Winter parties

The longest night of the year is called the solstice.
In the northern hemisphere, it is on December 21st.
In the south, it is on June 21st.

Christmas lights

At Christmas, the birth of Christ is celebrated in many different ways in Christian countries around the world. Lots of Christmas traditions are linked to ancient midwinter ceremonies. In Sweden, Christmas celebrations start on December 13th, when girls wear a headdress topped with candles, and boys dress as star boys, carrying star wands. The stars and the candles represent the coming of the sun and the melting of the winter snow.

New Year

New Year is celebrated in different winter months around the world. The Tibetan people celebrate their New Year, called Losar, in February. They hold a parade with 1,001 twinkling lanterns and candles. In New Zealand, the Maori people traditionally celebrate their New Year, called Matariki, in June. They sing songs, dance, and clean their homes to signal a new beginning.

Winter fires

Traditional winter parties often include bonfires. The people of the Shetland Islands off the northern coast of Scotland have a big bonfire party on January 26th called Up Helly Aa. Hundreds of years ago, the Vikings who lived on the islands started the Up Helly Aa bonfire ceremony because they thought the fire would help to scare away the long, cold nights of winter.

Snow fun

In February, two million people visit the Japanese city of Sapporo for the Yuki Matsuri snow festival. They come to see teams from all over the world carve amazing snow and ice sculptures of animals, buildings, trees, and figures. There are even slides made of snow for children to play on.

Paint the winter

Here are some ideas for making winter pictures.

Chilly colors

Blue, white, and gray are good colors for winter pictures. They are called cold colors, and they remind people of icy winter days.

Light on dark

Try using dark-colored background paper for winter night pictures. Light colors look extra bright on top of a dark background, so it's a good way to show shiny lights like the ones on this Christmas tree.

When you paint shadows on snow, use pale blue. It looks much more realistic than gray or black!

24

Making snow

Here are two ways to add falling snow to your pictures. Practice on some scrap paper before you try them on your finished paintings. Make sure the paintings are completely dry before you put the snow on top of them.

Potato chip snow

Potato chip snow

Scrunch up a potato chip bag. Dab it into white poster paint mixed on an old plate. Then dab it lightly onto a picture to make a snowstorm.

Toothbrush snow

Dip an old toothbrush into white poster paint and hold it with the bristles facing down over the picture. Run your finger along the bristles toward you to make the paint spray out.

Toothbrush snow

25

Make a piece of winter

Make an edible necklace for hungry winter birds, and a pretty snowflake to stick on your window.

Birdfood necklace

It is hard for birds to find food in a cold winter when plants and insects die. Put out food for them high up where they can eat it safely, away from cats. For this necklace, you will need a bag of peanuts in their shells, a strong needle, and some strong thread.

1. Cut a long length of thread. Knot one end and thread it through the needle.

2. Push the needle through the middle of each peanut shell, one by one, pulling it down to the knot at the bottom.

3. When you have enough peanuts, tie the ends of the thread together to make a necklace.

4. Hang the necklace on the branch of a tree or bush so you can see it from your window. Watch the birds come to feed on your tasty present!

A paper snowflake

Once you have made your first paper snowflake, you will want to make lots in different shapes and sizes! Tape them onto your window or make them out of cardboard and attach them to colored paper. You will need scissors, a pencil, and colored paper or cardboard.

1. Draw around something circle-shaped, such as a plate or cup. Cut around the circle you have drawn.

2. Fold the circle in half. Then fold it into three parts as shown.

3. Cut little pieces out of the straight edges, and a little more out of the curved edge.

4. Unfold the paper to see your snowflake. Now make a different one!

Be a winter scientist

Discover some winter science by
finding out the secrets of ice.

Wildlife watch

Explore the winter wildlife outside your window. All you need
is a notebook or paper, some colored pencils or pens, and
some birdfood. If you can, borrow some binoculars.

Ask an adult if you can put
some birdfood outside a
window. Try breadcrumbs,
bacon rind, or a bird
feeder full of peanuts.

The best time to watch
birds is in the morning or
at dusk, when they
come to feed.

Draw each bird you see, and
color it in. Later on, use your
drawing to find out the bird's
name in a bird book. Label
your drawings with the time
and date you made them.

Secrets of ice

Ice is frozen water. Experiment with freezing fruit juice, which is mostly water, to find out two ice secrets. You will need two plastic cups, a pen, a refrigerator, and a freezer compartment.

1. Fill the two cups with the same amount of juice (about half full is best). Use the pen to mark the level of the juice on the outside of each cup.

2. Put one cup in the refrigerator and one in the freezer.

3. The next day, look at your cups. Has all the juice frozen? Look at the juice level in each container. Is it the same as yesterday?

Let the frozen juice warm up a little to soften, and then eat it with a spoon!

Did you get these results?

Water has to be at a temperature of 32 °F (0 °C) to freeze. Your refrigerator shouldn't be that cold, but your freezer should be. Water expands (gets bigger) when it freezes, so the frozen juice should be higher up in the cup.

Words to remember

Antarctica The frozen land at the far south of the world.

Arctic The frozen sea at the far north of the world.

blizzard A heavy snowstorm.

deciduous tree A tree that loses its leaves in the winter.

equator The imaginary line around the middle of Earth.

evaporate To disappear into the air.

evergreen tree A tree that keeps its leaves year-round.

frost Ice crystals that are made when the weather gets so cold that water vapor in the air freezes and settles on the ground.

hemispheres The northern and southern halves of Earth.

hibernate To hide away and rest during the winter months. Polar bears hibernate in the winter.

migrate To journey from a cold part of the world to a warmer part of the world for the winter, and to make a return journey in the spring.

North Pole The point on Earth that is the farthest north. It is located on sea that is always frozen.

snowflake A group of ice crystals stuck together to make a six-sided shape.

South Pole The point on Earth that is the farthest south. It is on land that is always frozen.

temperature How hot or cold something is.

thermometer A tube with liquid inside that is used to measure temperature.

winter solstice The shortest day of the year. In the southern hemisphere, it is June 21st. In the northern hemisphere, it is December 21st.

Index

Antarctic 7, 18, 19
Arctic 18, 19

bats 17
bears 17, 19
birds 8, 18, 26
blizzards 11

cows 15

Earth 4, 5, 6
equator 4, 5, 6
evaporation 13

farms 14, 15
foxes 16
frost 11

gardens 12

hibernation 17

ice 10, 11
insects 8, 19

leaves 8, 12, 13

mice 16
migration 18
musk oxen 18

North Pole 5, 7

owls 18

plants 8, 12

rabbits 17
reindeer 18

sheep 15
soil 14
solstice 22
squirrels 16
sun 4, 5, 6

temperature 9
trees 8, 12, 13

weasels 17